C000001276

© 2016 by Barnardo's

All rights reserved. No part of this book may be
reproduced in any form without written permission
of the copyright owners. All images in this book have
been reproduced with the knowledge and prior consent
of the persons concerned, and no responsibility is
accepted by producer, publisher or printer for any
infringement of copyright or otherwise, arising from the
contents of this publication. Every effort has been made
to ensure that credits accurately comply with information
supplied. We apologise for any inaccuracies that may
have occured and will resolve inaccurate or missing
information in a subsequent reprinting of the book.

Barnardo House
Tanners Lane
Barkingside
Ilford
Essex IG6 1QG
Telephone: 020 8550 8822
www.barnardos.org.uk

ISBN: 978-1-907645-07-5

Design: David O'Sullivan, Barnardo's
david.osullivan@barnardos.org.uk

Editor: Diane Church
diane.church@virgin.net

Printed by CPI

This book is dedicated to the memory of all the children
that Barnardo's has supported over the last 150 years who
are no longer with us, in particular to Alan Dearman, who
passed away in February 2016 and was such an inspiring
advocate for Barnardo's all of his life.

Registered Charity Numbers 216250 and SC037605.
Barnardo's adheres to the Fundraising Promise and
Fundraising Standards Board guidelines.

give with confidence

Contents

Foreword

©www.royalimages.co.uk

❝ Reading the stories of so many different people in this new book *Barnardo's Voices*, in such diverse circumstances, helps us appreciate the scope and importance of Barnardo's work over the last 150 years.

Sometimes, Barnardo's is part of a young person's life for a brief period to help them through a crisis. Other times, Barnardo's provides sustained support to ensure a safe childhood, a more stable family or a stronger community for children to grow up in.

Barnardo's Voices includes the story of Jim Jarvis, the first street child Dr Thomas Barnardo met in Victorian London in 1867. It also features the stories of children who grew up in Barnardo's care in the 1930s, '40s and '50s, as well as some of the tens of thousands of children, young people and families the charity supports in local communities today.

The clear message throughout is that, whatever its role, Barnardo's has consistently protected and cared for the UK's most vulnerable children over the last 150 years.

As Patron, I am very proud to be associated with this worthwhile and valuable cause and I sincerely hope that Barnardo's will continue to be there for the generations of children in need in the future.

_____

ELIZABETH R.

9

Introduction

❝ For the first time in our history, we have brought the 'voices' of Barnardo's children – past and present – from across the UK together in this inspirational and historical book.

From Victorian street boys and girls who were rescued from London's East End to the most disadvantaged children, young people and their families that we work with today, *Barnardo's Voices* is a testament to the charity's incredible achievements over the last 150 years.

We believe every child has the potential to thrive. And we know whatever the odds against them are, children always seem to find a way to cope – if they're given the chance.

The children featured in *Barnardo's Voices* have experienced the most traumatic or troubling childhoods. What they also share is the achievement of having turned their lives around with support from Barnardo's.

When Thomas Barnardo first came to London in 1866, he was appalled by the human suffering he witnessed. He dedicated his life to transforming the lives of London's most vulnerable children – whether they were sick, starving or destitute and whatever their physical ability, ethnicity or religious beliefs. Thomas Barnardo made a promise – that no child would ever be turned away.

Alongside his wife Syrie, his work was revolutionary. They established small-scale 'cottage homes' with house parents to emulate a homely environment and to best nurture children's needs. They pioneered 'boarding out', a Victorian equivalent to fostering, whereby children could live with families rather than in large-scale institutions. They set up training schools, such as Watts Naval Training School and Goldings, where young people could learn a trade. They campaigned and advocated for children's rights and established the charity I am honoured to lead today.

Barnardo's history is intertwined with the UK's social development. Over the last 150 years we have responded to the demands of the times, such as social deprivation, mass unemployment and war. For instance, Bill Heath found home and comfort in Barnardo's when his injured ex-serviceman father was unable to care for him after the First World War. Inge Ball found safety in Barnardo's Village at Barkingside when she escaped Nazi Germany in 1938 as one of the Kindertransport children. And today, we're supporting the Al-Ahmed family who are refugees from Syria and have recently settled in Northern Ireland as their home country is torn apart by violence and fear.

Thomas Barnardo couldn't have foreseen the future, but I believe he'd be very proud of what we're doing today.

We no longer run orphanages and only have a few specialist children's homes. We work across the UK with around 248,000 vulnerable children, young people and families each year, providing 996 specialist services in local communities. These include: services for disabled children and young people; preventative and intensive family support; advice and time-out for young carers; support for care leavers and those affected by child sexual exploitation; as well as help into education, training and employment. But there is no room for complacency. We are determined to continue making a positive difference to children's lives.

I have the opportunity to travel around the country meeting our staff who deliver these services. I call them our front line 'angels'.

Working with such amazing people is humbling. So many *Barnardo's Voices* talk of their Barnardo's worker – that special someone they had to turn to, who believed in them when they had been abandoned or given up on by the rest of the world.

Vera Back, who was in Barnardo's care in the 1960s, remembers her social worker Mrs Couttes. Fifty years on, Vera says: "She was the first person to show me there are nice people out there." Vera has stayed in touch with Mrs Couttes throughout her life and was herself inspired to become a senior child care manager. Paolo, who recently adopted three-year-old Joshua, feels incredibly grateful for the care and expertise he has received from his support worker, Irene, in making his family complete. "She was fantastic from the beginning. Her enthusiasm, knowledge and training were amazing."

Positive change has an on-going impact. Many of the *Barnardo's Voices* in this book talk of 'wanting to give something back', of 'making a contribution' or 'helping others' as a result of their own experiences. When someone is in crisis, they remember the belief someone showed in them.

Care leaver Andrew was virtually abandoned on his 16th birthday but, with Barnardo's support, he is now settled and living independently. Not only that, but he is using his experiences to help others by writing a self-help guide for the next generation of care leavers. He is also fundraising for Barnardo's.

John Spencer, now aged 79, was in Barnardo's care for two years when his mother had four children under six and his dad was doing war work in the 1940s. He still supports Barnardo's today. His quote captures Barnardo's belief in children, both past and present:

"Barnardo's was there for me when I needed it – as it has been for tens of thousands of others. Such support – at the right time – can make the difference between success and failure in life. Fortunately I was one of the lucky ones."

Directly and indirectly, millions of people around the world have benefitted from Barnardo's work over the past 150 years. Barnardo's has transformed lives and, in some cases, saved lives.

Those in *Barnardo's Voices* measure success in different ways. For some, it is having their own loving, secure family. For others, it is reaching the top of their chosen profession. And then there are those for whom peace of mind, or just being able to walk down the street without having a panic attack, is just as important.

Barnardo's will be needed more than ever in the next ten years. The challenges will be as vast as they will be complex. Desperate children, young people and their families will be looking for the hand of support that will make the difference between their success or their failure to cope with their challenges. We will be there for them.

Thank you for your belief in children and for your generous support. The gifts we receive from our supporters – be they cash or donations to shops or gifts left in Wills – are vital to funding our on-going valuable work. Your donations support the *Barnardo's Voices* of today and enable us to plan innovative new services for the voices of tomorrow.

By working together, we truly believe that there is no obstacle, however large it is, a child cannot overcome. Thank you for sharing this belief too – past, present and future.

JAVED KHAN, CHIEF EXECUTIVE
BARNARDO'S

Voices of

COURAGE

“ When I was 15, my mum and stepdad (who I didn't get on with) emigrated leaving me behind. I went into a care home in the North East and was diagnosed with depression. I felt suicidal and started self-harming. I was also in a foster home for a month but didn't like it.

At 16, I moved to Leeds to go to college and was referred to Barnardo's. I moved into supported housing and they helped me massively. There's a 24 hour call line I can use if I need it. They are always there for me. My support worker Amanda is like an angel. I didn't get along with my mum. At Barnardo's, I'm a lot happier in every way. Now I'm studying health and social care, maths and psychology. I will be applying to go to university but I'm not sure what to study yet.

EMILY, AGED 18

ALWAYS

66 I was born in Cyprus. My grandmother agreed to raise me on the condition that my mother went to live and work in England. We lived in a house that had one room. We ate, slept and bathed in that room.

When I was eight, I was sent to England and met by a woman who said she was my mother. I also met my younger sister for the first time. She didn't speak Greek and I didn't speak English.

My mother was living with another man who abused my sister and me. Mother didn't believe me and I had no one else to tell. She was also physically abusive to us. Then one day she said we were going to live in a children's home and there would be plenty of other children to play with. I couldn't wait to get there.

When I grew older, Barnardo's sent me to college to learn confectionery skills. Barnardo's helped me all the way. I can never repay them. I got a job at the Cumberland Hotel and even worked on a birthday cake for Prince Charles. Then, at 19, I moved to Norway after meeting some new friends. I met my husband there, an Englishman working for NATO.

I believe in God. I think if it wasn't for my faith, I'd be in a mental home or would have got rid of myself. Barnardo's has always been there for me. I know it's not been a bed of roses, but for me, I can only say thank God they were there. I've always kept in touch, like a lifeline.

HELEN SIMPSON

"As a young, Pakistani, ex-Muslim, gay man fleeing for my life on the streets of Newcastle, I only allowed myself one thought. 'It is better to be hungry and free than full and imprisoned'.

From the age of 12, I knew I was going to have to run away. I knew two things to be true: first that I was gay and second that my parents were abusive for fear of *Izaat* – which roughly translated means 'honour'.

I fled. I fled as fast and as far as I could get and I will never forget the numbness that followed me that night. Looking back now, I realise just how vulnerable I was: homeless, naïve and numb. A week later, I was introduced to a Barnardo's service known as Crash Pad, which would save my life.

I was shown more dignity and love in one week there than I had experienced in 18 years. I was fortunate enough to enter the heart and home of Sharon Dent. She clothed and fed me, drove me to and from university every year. She made me the man that I am today. With every kind word and every gentle hug, she washed away oceans of resentment.

And so you see, I am no longer afraid of my family. I've lived the last three years as if every day was my first, and in all honesty, I didn't expect to make it this far.

MICHAEL FARAH, AGED 22

19

DIGNITY

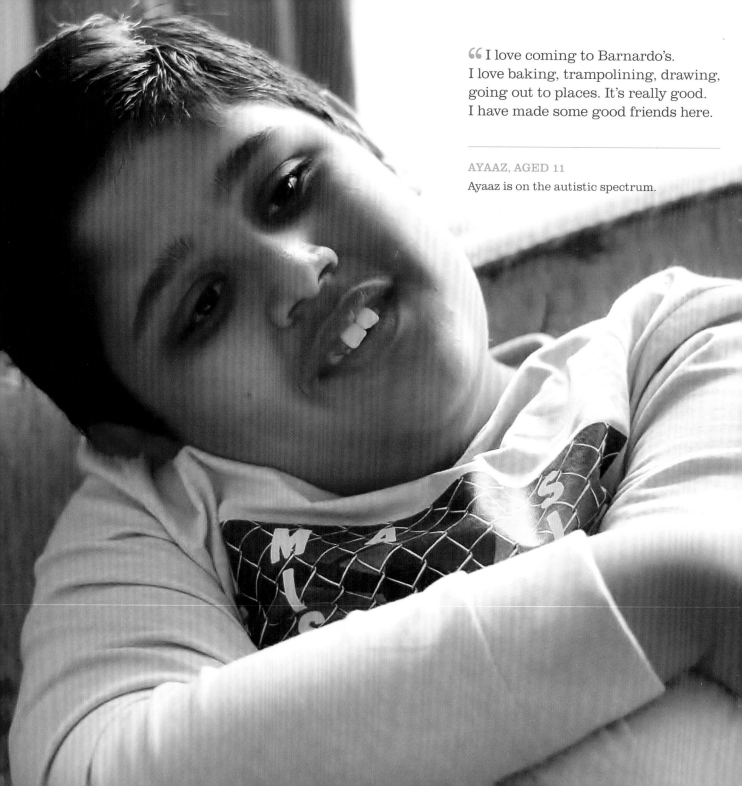

**" I love coming to Barnardo's.
I love baking, trampolining, drawing,
going out to places. It's really good.
I have made some good friends here.**

AYAAZ, AGED 11
Ayaaz is on the autistic spectrum.

ENABLES

“ Barnardo's support has made a huge difference in our lives. It enables me – not only to have time to myself – but also to spend time with my other children. Barnardo's has been brilliant. They really understand my son and his needs. Ayaaz loves coming here and I really value the service.

SURAYA

Mother of Ayaaz.

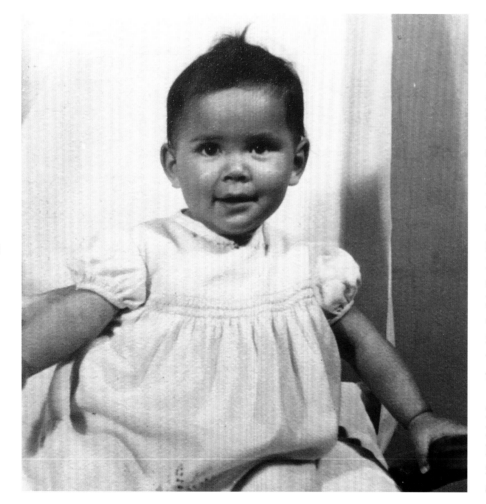

“ There was always a presence of Barnardo's in my life while I was growing up. My mother was Scottish and my father Indian, so I was a dual-heritage baby. My mother didn't want me, so I was left at the hospital. From my records, I know I came into Barnardo's care when I was about six weeks old. I was boarded out to a white English family who had three boys and wanted a girl. I was never adopted. In those days 'mixed race' or 'children of colour' were not deemed adoptable. We were placed with families to see if we fitted in.

My teen years were difficult. I really struggled with not knowing my birth family and my foster family never spoke about my dual-heritage. I wish

FAMILY

we'd discussed it. Barnardo's tried to answer my questions and I think they've learnt from those times and do things differently now.

Although I left home at 17, my foster family are still my family today and the boys think of me as their sister.

I later decided to train as a counsellor and therapist. I want to make life better for me and other people and that's a direct result of how Barnardo's shaped and influenced me.

I don't know where I'd be without them. I was a destitute child and they didn't turn me away. Barnardo's was my first family.

JEAN SHEFALIE- HOLLIS

" The most difficult challenge was getting off drugs. I was taking them from the age of 16. I was still going to college but didn't turn up very often. I wasn't very hopeful when I left care. I trusted no one. I was sofa surfing for two to three months then one day my friend told me to go. I went to Barnardo's at 9am that morning.

JACK, AGED 19

Barnardo's runs 24 leaving care services across the UK which aim to bridge the gap for looked after children between leaving care and independent living. These services worked with 2,800 people last year. Our other services worked with an additional 500 care leavers.

HOPEFUL

66 Through Barnardo's I've had so many opportunities: like getting to London to see a show and meeting politicians to try and make things better for care leavers coming behind us – not every kid gets to do that.

Now I've baked a cake for Barnardo's 150th anniversary party at Buckingham Palace and was presented to the Duchess of Cornwall at the Garden Party. I can't believe it, I'm still dreaming. Barnardo's always encourages me. No one ever once put me down. Barnardo's is awesome.

ABI, AGED 20
Abi was in care from 14 and moved to Barnardo's Leaving Care service when she was 17. She studied catering at college.

ENCOURAGES

DUTY

Henry Hickey was born on 16 May 1893 and spent time at a Barnardo's home before being migrated to Canada in March 1902. Like so many other child migrants, Henry responded to Britain's call for troops at the start of World War One and joined the 4th Canadian Battalion.

Throughout the war, Sergeant Hickey – as he became known – showed a remarkable devotion to duty. His bravery and intelligence led him to be recommended for the Victoria Cross (VC) medal by his commanding officer.

The VC is the army's highest award in the UK honours system and is awarded for gallantry 'in the face of the enemy'. Hickey was recommended for the medal after he volunteered to recover two trench mortars belonging to his battalion. They had been abandoned in a ditch the previous day. However this excursion, which promised Hickey certain death due to heavy gunfire, led him to discover a shorter and safer route from which men in the reserve trenches could be brought to the frontline.

As Barnardo's annual report for 1919 said: 'It was a discovery which saved many lives at a moment when every life was of the greatest value. Time and time and time again, at the risk of his own life as he went back and forth, he guided party after party up to the trenches by this route'.

Tragically, Hickey was killed in battle before being formally presented with the medal but he did receive the DCM (Distinguished Conduct Medal) – an extremely high level award for bravery in battle and on land.

During World War One, 520 known Barnardo's Boys died in action and a memorial plaque was erected at the charity's then-headquarters in Stepney to commemorate 'the gallant dead'.

On Armistice day, 11 November 1918, there were more than 10,700 known Barnardo's Boys in the armed services, 22 of whom had been awarded army commissions during the war.

HENRY HICKEY

27

PROTECTING

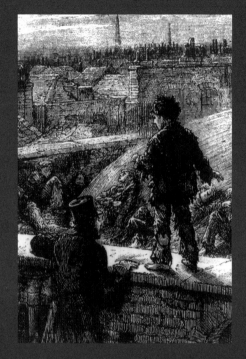

In 1867, 21-year-old Thomas Barnardo encountered a destitute street child in Victorian London called Jim Jarvis. At the time, Barnardo was running a ragged school but after meeting Jim, he decided to dedicate the rest of his life to caring for the most vulnerable children.

"He had a small, spare, stunted frame and he was clad in miserable rags – loathsome from their dirt – without either shirt, shoes or stockings," said Barnardo. "I could see here was a phase of poverty far beneath anything from which the noisy, wayward ragged school had familiarised me."

Jarvis took Barnardo on a tour of London's back streets showing him starving boys sleeping on open roofs without any protection from the cold and without any support or care in their lives.

"Looking down...at 11 upturned faces, white with cold and hunger, a sight to be burned in my memory, and to recur again and again..."

The young philanthropist immediately took in Jim Jarvis. Within a year, he had opened his first home for street boys in London's East End. Here he provided accommodation, an education and training, protecting children from harm and enabling them to become independent, responsible adults.

JIM JARVIS
Jim was the first of more than 35,000 children whom Barnardo supported in his lifetime.

"I was in care from four and was introduced to Barnardo's Children's Rights Service when I was ten.

In 2009 I became a participation worker at the project – helping other young people who are in care or in the process of leaving care.

Those were great times. There were some amazing young people and together we knew we could achieve anything. For every 10 people we helped, another 20 would benefit and so it would go on – it was like a ripple effect.

With young people, it's easier to push them away and let them get lost in the system. The main thing is giving them a voice. When they feel like they have a voice, it empowers them to do more and more.

By building on small goals it helps them see the bigger picture.

JEROME HARVEY-AGYEI, AGED 26
Jerome was an advocate at the London Children's Rights Service in East London for seven years.

RIPPLE

PARADISE

" Without Barnardo's help, I don't know how we would have managed or what would have happened to me. I don't remember much about him, but when my dad had come back from World War One, he'd lost an arm. He sold rags, then he'd go to the pub and drink the money he'd made. We slept rough, in barns and on park benches. When I went to Barnardo's and lay in a bed, looking up at a ceiling instead of the sky, I thought I was in paradise.

I was boarded out (fostered) in several homes. The first one, when I was about five, was a farm in Norfolk. There were two big horses and I loved it.

I went on to be a bit of a 'Jack of all trades' working in mining and civil engineering. At one time, I had 14 men working for my company. But I was always interested in farming, so when I retired I bought a small farm of my own.

BILL HEATH

66 I went into Barnardo's the day before my second birthday and I still remember it vividly. When I was six, I was shown a lady who looked like Elizabeth Taylor and was told she was my mother. My mother and father had got back together again. She had a babe in arms, so I now had three brothers.

Within six months, I was taken back to Barnardo's. Life at home had been terrible. My mum just turned and walked away. I didn't have any of my brothers with me this time. No one to answer my questions.

I had a social worker, Mrs Couttes, who was super. She was always interested in me. She is now in her 90s and I still see her. I aspired to be like her. She was the first person to show me there are nice people out there.

I had a bumpy start, but I've been lucky in life. I am now retired, married and we have a son and a daughter. All my life, I've tried to help children. My daughter is a social worker. When I stopped work, I was a strategic child care manager in early years development at Somerset County Council.

Without Barnardo's, I don't know what would have happened to me. It wasn't perfect, but it provided me with a safety net. They did their best for me.

VERA BACK

31

ASPIRED

“ I was a young carer for my brother when I joined Barnardo's Young Carers. About six or seven years ago my mum's health began to deteriorate. We didn't know what was wrong, but she would be very ill at times. Mum was diagnosed with MS just over a year ago. It was hard. I was in the middle of my exams. I didn't have friends in school. I was very anxious and worried a lot. I was always concerned about home. When my mum and dad split, my dad retreated into his shell. So I look after his house for him too.

Barnardo's took me out and let me meet new people. I've had some really good times. I now have a group of friends I can really speak to and they just get it. If Barnardo's wasn't there, I wouldn't be here.

When I started at Barnardo's, I was in a black place. I get involved now – it has helped me branch out. I'm doing my A Levels and planning to join the Royal Navy.

LIBERTY, AGED 18
Carer to her brother who is on the autistic spectrum, her dad and her mum who has multiple sclerosis (MS).

INVOLVED

Voices of

HOPE
_____

ACCESS

66 I am the second person from Meadows School* to go to university. I had a very difficult time as a child and teenager and from the ages of 13-15, I was not in education. My parents tried to get me a special needs school place, but were denied. Eventually Meadows was recommended. I was 15 when I started there. Before then, I wasn't able to step outside of my house. When I went there, I felt as though I finally had a chance to access an education. I had felt until then that it would probably never happen. Now I'm doing a degree at the University of Sussex and I have my own flat.

KAY, AGED 19

* Meadows School in Kent run by Barnardo's is a special residential school for young people with severe emotional and behavioural difficulties.

ENERGY

66 Barnado's afforded me the opportunity to develop life skills. Living in a diverse community of children, I became accepting and respectful of others. Due to some negative experiences, I have become an advocate for kindness.

I never knew why my brother and I were placed in Barnardo's and there was a sense of shame when I was a child about being in care. I felt unwanted and unloved.

You can't wash that away, but you can turn it into a force for something more positive. Barnardo's has been a prism of light in my life: an energy that has made me burn brighter. I studied psychology at college and then I did a masters in counselling and now I am a speciality nurse. I've always tried to be compassionate to those I meet. Having seen suffering and sadness, I think it is very important to help other people.

I felt a very strong need to be a mother and I've told my four children about my childhood. They were shocked and have so much respect for me – for everything I've gone through. They've told me I'm a good

mother, which is the best thing anyone could possibly say to me. My children mean the world to me.

CHERYL CHAMBERS

" I've been in foster care since I was four years old and during that time, I've had four different placements.

On my 18th birthday, when my foster placement came to an end, I came to Barnardo's Supported Lodging in Leeds.

I was taken to meet a lady called Maureen who is a Barnardo's supported lodgings provider. I was a little bit nervous, but Maureen was lovely and the other lad living there was really welcoming.

It's been a year now and I'm so pleased I moved in. Maureen is caring and loving and is helping me to get ready for when I move on in life. I'm really glad I found Barnardo's, they've really helped.

TYLER, AGED 19

WELCOMING

“ We'd wanted children for a long time. I was an actor and when I was in a panto with a cast of children – that tipped me over the edge. It was Christmas time and it was then that friends suggested we should get in touch with Barnardo's about adoption.

In two weeks we had more information from Barnardo's than all the councils put together. Our social worker then is very much part of our family now.

Your whole world changes overnight when you adopt. Things are so vastly different – but in a good way. It has not been without its challenges though. Barnardo's has provided moral support and helpful tips.

I've now stopped acting and work for Barnardo's as a family finder – advising other people who are going through the adoption process.

IAN (QUOTED) AND PAUL WITH THEIR SONS
Ian and Paul adopted two brothers aged two and four. The boys had previously been fostered with separate families and they are now reunited permanently.

SUPPORT

" I've come through life well. I've had my hard times, but more than my share of good times too.

I was only in Barnardo's for about two years in the war. My mum had four children under six and my dad was on war work.

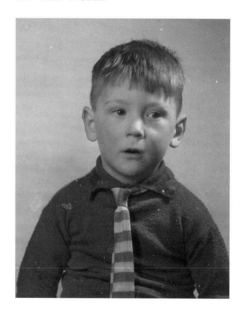

I'm an analytical chemist by trade and have mainly worked in environmental science. For years I worked in the energy industry, analysing the emissions of power stations, then later I worked for Bournemouth University.

I retired sixteen years ago but keep busy: raising money for charities through the Rotary Club and, as my wife died of Alzheimer's four years ago, I now lead on recruiting volunteers for dementia research in my area. In fact, I'm the Wessex Champion for *Join Dementia* research in my region.

Barnardo's was there for me when I needed it – as it has been for tens of thousands of others. Such support – at the right time – can make

the difference between success and failure in life. Fortunately I was one of the lucky ones.

JOHN SPENCER

HEART

"I was in and out of Barnardo's care all my childhood. At 18, I signed up for the navy as I was so institutionalised. I lasted for two years, but then came out.

At times, my life has been a real struggle and I've been completely alone in the world.

Since 1997, I've worked for Southampton City Children's Services in various roles and am now a qualified personal advisor helping care leavers in the transition to adulthood.

Barnardo's showed me that you never give up on young people, even if they cause you frustration, stress and anxiety. I try and follow my heart – by turning what was a negative childhood and teenage life into a positive.

JACKIE MATTHEWS

" It was very lonely when I left care. I was not used to coming home and not having anyone around. I was working in retail when I started living independently, but soon realised I didn't want to do it long term.

Every day I applied for work and apprenticeships, just for something…anything… to do. My personal advisor told me that Barnardo's was helping young people get into apprenticeships.

A Barnardo's employment training and skills worker supported me, helping with CV and letter writing and interview techniques. I then applied for the role I'm doing now and was successfully shortlisted.

I've been a business and admin apprentice at Barnardo's Independent Visitor project for over a year now and have achieved so much during that time.

I co-interviewed Barnardo's Chief Executive, Javed Khan, about the charity's new ten-year strategy. I've helped facilitate training sessions for volunteers and have encouraged and helped young people to speak in front of volunteers to share their stories. I'm currently producing a cookbook for care leavers with 150 recipes to celebrate Barnardo's 150th anniversary.

In September, I'm starting a degree in Early Childhood at the University of East London. I'm ready to start this new adventure. It's been a long time coming, but my experience at Barnardo's has given me hope. I'm really proud of what I've achieved and I can't wait to start a new chapter.

CATARINA FERNANDO, AGED 22

45

ACHIEVED

George (2) were admitted to Barnardo's in 1898 after their father died and their mother struggled to make ends meet. At that time, Fred's height was just over 4 feet – above average for his age at the time – but not exceptional.

The following year, the boys joined thousands of other English disadvantaged and impoverished children who were found homes in Canada. At that time, Barnardo's – and many other leading agencies caring for the country's most vulnerable children – believed that an outdoor life learning agricultural skills was much better than the urban poverty and exploitation they faced on the streets of London.

Frederick Kempster was born on 13 April 1889 in west London where his father worked as a milk carrier. He was the sixth of seven children. The two youngest boys Fred (8) and his brother

By 1904, aged 15, Fred was returned to England due to

a congenital knee problem. This was the onset of his uncontrolled growth that would shape the rest of his life. Fred's development into a 'giant' had begun.

In the spring of 1911, Kempster was the tallest man

WELL-ADJUSTED

in a parade of giants – planned as part of the celebrations for the coronation of King George V. The attention he received from the press and public must have been Fred's first indication that his unusual height might be a means to make a living.

He got a job with Astley & Co, an American Circus at Chigwell in Essex and when he visited Barnardo's that year, he reported that he was doing well.

"Fred loved people. It is said he was a happy, well-adjusted chap who liked to talk to the public," said his great-nephew Jim Kempster.

"He does not appear to have been victimised or outcast because of his unusual size."

Fred became famous all over the country and was known as the *English Giant*.

"By the autumn of 1913, Fred stood slightly over 7ft 9in, and his picture – taken while visiting family in Bath – appeared in newspapers all over the world," continued Jim. Fred continued to tour the UK as part of a travelling fair for the rest of his life, but sadly he contracted pneumonia and died on 15 April 1918 aged 29.

FRED KEMPSTER

Fred Kempster was in the *Guinness Book of Records* from 1967 to 1993 as one of the tallest men in England, where he was reported to have measured 8ft 4 inches at the time of his death. Photographic evidence, however, suggests that his height may have been nearer 7ft 9 inches.

TRUST

❝ About six years ago we were in Pakistan with our family and we saw orphaned children living outside in the cold and wanted to do something to help.

When we came back to England, we applied to Barnardo's to become foster carers. It was the best thing we have ever done.

We live with our two sons aged 25 and 11, our daughter, her husband and their one-year-old son.

We currently have two unaccompanied asylum-seeking children living with us. They are from Afghanistan and Tunisia and are both aged 16. When any unaccompanied child refugee arrives here, they are very traumatised. They're very happy to have finally made it, but you can see in their eyes that there's a hurt and loss inside them. They haven't seen their families or loved ones for several years and have witnessed and experienced terrible things.

The lads trusted no one when they arrived. One of those living with us was dropped 80 miles from his home in the desert and walked to Europe over many months – very daunting for an 11-year-old. Once the lads are settled in school and in a routine, they start to feel more secure and, with that, they become more confident. My 11-year-old son is good at kicking a ball around with them. Little things like that can help a lot.

Barnardo's is a very professional organisation and they keep us updated with everything, including all our training needs, which are vital. They're always there to provide all the help we need.

ABDUL AND ZAHIDA

FANTASTIC

"I adopted Joshua* on my own when he was three. It was very tough at the beginning. I was aware of some of the challenges and I had planned for them as best I could, but it's difficult to plan how to handle the emotional issues that a child will bring and I didn't know about all the resources available to me. The first year was very difficult.

Joshua can't express his emotions well and he has difficulty with speech and language. When he joined the reception year it was very hard for him, and he was bringing all his bad behaviour to school.

The local authority put me in touch with Barnardo's and our support worker, Irene, was fantastic from the beginning. Her enthusiasm, knowledge and training were amazing.

There have been tremendous improvements in terms of Joshua's attention span and his understanding of feelings and how to deal with them. Separation has always been an issue, but now he's much better at handling it. I hope that one day Joshua will be able to understand the significance of the education, health and care plan that Barnardo's has helped put in place for him.

51

PAOLO

Single parent, adopted Joshua when he was three.

* Name changed to protect identity.

66 When Peter* applied to be on the Barnardo's Families Matter programme at the prison, we didn't really know what it was, but it has turned out to be great.

During the extended family visits we can be together as a family. Peter can walk around with Toby*, lift him and crawl on the floor with him. There's the opportunity for that bond to grow, which is so important.

As a mummy, that's what you want – for that bond to be there. When Toby arrives and his dad lifts him up, I just burst with pride. The Barnardo's staff here really care. They really empathise and give us the opportunity to talk.

BOND

When I think about how far we've come and what we've had to go through to get here, it's been hard, but I couldn't say enough about the programme and what Barnardo's has done for us. It has turned our lives around.

SARAH*

Sarah and her partner Peter from Northern Ireland are parents of two-year-old toddler Toby. Peter is currently in HMP Maghaberry serving a four year sentence.

Around 200,000 children are affected by parental imprisonment across England and Wales.

* Names changed to protect identities.

FRIEND

66 I'm a volunteer mentor. When I first met Arun*, he had little self-confidence. We meet monthly and do things he likes to do. We play football, have a takeaway... he chooses, it's Arun's time.

Over the last two years, I've seen real changes in him. He even introduced me to a mate, saying: 'My friend Kevin – he's the only friend I've got.'

I don't think people should be the sum product of their parents. Some people don't have very good parents – that's just the way of the world. I think they should be given the opportunity to break free from that.

I do it because I enjoy it. It keeps my feet on the ground.

KEVIN

Volunteer mentor to Arun, who was taken into foster care when he was eight due to domestic abuse.

Name changed to protect identity.

❝ When I first met Drew at my foster family, we both felt comfortable straight away.

He is an actor and we both like theatre. I'm currently doing an extended diploma at the Brit School, so he'll look around for different offers on theatre tickets. We also go to the cinema quite often.

When we meet we'll talk about our social lives. I know I can confide in Drew and he'll do his best to understand and talk about his own experiences. It's mostly about acting and performing, and he's very motivating. Even though we only meet once a month, it's enough for us to keep up to date.

I like going out with Drew because it's different to being out with my teenage friends and it's often in a new kind of social environment.

To be a good independent visitor, you just need to be yourself and not try to be a social worker. Drew is very straight up and real and I respect that about him.

I hope we've built up enough of a relationship to carry on meeting as I get older. There are few people I plan to repay in the future, but Drew is one of those people.

MOTIVATING

57

SOLOMON, AGED 17

Only three per cent of looked after children have an independent visitor. Barnardo's is campaigning for more.

Independent visitor Drew is an actor and Barnardo's volunteer.

VOLUNTEER

❝ I've been volunteering at the Barnardo's shop in Omagh for a year and a half. I first got involved as part of the Millennium Volunteers but after that ended I stayed on, just because I enjoy it.

I volunteer every Saturday and every other Sunday. When you're serving in the shop you can really see that you're making a connection with people and making a difference to someone's day and that's important to me.

I hope to go on to uni and study law and I think the experience will be really useful. It's also nice to think the work I'm doing in the shop goes back into the charity and is making a difference to a child somewhere.

SHANE MORIARTY, AGED 19

Voices of

ACHIEVEMENT

SUPERHERO

“ At Barnardo's, I can just be myself and feel accepted. I can be who I am and forget my stresses. I really want to come every time and I go like a bullet. It's given me so much confidence and it's helped me control my autism. I can speak in public without stuttering and fidgeting. By speaking out on issues like self-directed support, decision-making and disability awareness training, it means I can help make a difference for children younger than me. I can make it better for their futures. It makes me feel like I can really make change for the good, like I'm a superhero!

JAMIE CURRAN, AGED 14

Jamie is on the autistic spectrum and attends Barnardo's Disabled Children and Young People's Participation Project, Northern Ireland, which supports and promotes the rights of children and young people with disabilities.

Wallace Ford was born Samuel Jones Grundy in Lancashire. He was admitted to Barnardo's in 1904 when he was six years old. A year later, he was sent as a child migrant to Canada. According to his own account, he ran away from home at the age of 11 and joined a vaudeville troupe.

In 1919, he played to full houses in Chicago for several months, before transferring to a successful run on Broadway.

His career was launched. Throughout the 1920s, Wallace became a regular Broadway performer.

He made a successful move to Hollywood and usually played tough, wise-cracking characters who had a friendly demeanour. He acted alongside many of the Hollywood greats: John Wayne, Joseph Cotton, Ingrid Bergman and Sidney Poitier, to name but a few.

PERFORMER

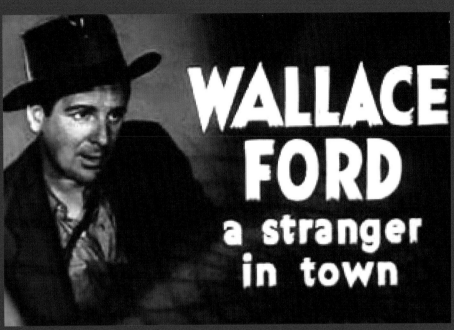

Wallace was a particular favourite of the director John Ford and appeared in many of his Westerns in a supporting role. His final performance was in a movie called *A Patch of Blue* in 1965, a controversial film for the time about inter-racial love, for which he received a Golden Laurel nomination.

Wallace was extremely proud of being a Barnardo Boy. He kept in contact with the charity throughout his adult life and there are photographs of him visiting the charity's headquarters in Stepney Causeway in East London.

SAMUEL GRUNDY

❝ I was sent to England from Trinidad when I was seven, as one of the 'Windrush' folk – citizens of the colonies were invited to Britain to help address worker shortages after the war. I came to join my mother and younger twin sisters. I arrived on 18 April 1955. My mother had left for the UK a couple of years earlier and she barely recognised me. We lived in west London in pretty rough conditions. It was difficult for her to manage, so she enquired about placing my younger sisters and me in Barnardo's care.

My mother was in contact and paid Barnardo's for our keep. She was training to be a nurse, to better herself, which was the reason she'd come to England in the first place.

CONTRIBUTION

I left school and applied for clerical jobs. One insurance company said that they would not employ 'coloured' people. I did get a job, but decided to join the army.

Because of my time in Barnardo's, I did exceedingly well. I spent 23 years in the military. Then, when I was 41, I joined the Surrey Constabulary and was awarded the *Baton of Honour* for outstanding contribution to the cause.

In the army and police I never had one ounce of trouble. I was always able to use my knack and wit, treating people as I'd wish to be treated. I owe that to life in Barnardo's.

CALVERT PETERS

BELIEVE

" There were happy times at home as a child. I remember going on holiday as a family and building sandcastles on the beach. We did everything together as a family.

Then when I was eight, things started to change. Mum stopped joining in. She wouldn't give us hugs and she started self harming. I went into the bathroom and saw that she had cut her wrists and was bleeding into the water. Mum is currently in hospital and doesn't live with us.

At Doncaster Young Carers, I didn't talk to my worker Wendy for ages. 'Yes' and 'no' was all I said.

Barnardo's helped me to believe in myself. I started to understand that I can have a life, I don't need to be at home 24/7. I'm part of the Young Carers Council now and I feel part of something. Before I didn't feel like I belonged anywhere.

Now I'm studying for my A Levels and am looking forward to starting at uni.

ROBYN, AGED 18

At Goldings training school, I was able to learn a trade as a printer and after finishing my apprenticeship at the age of 21, I worked as a compositor right up until retirement.

I was also a Wimbledon ball boy for three years running.

The final year was on Centre Court, which was brilliant.

I met my wife Jaqui in 1963 when she was 16 and I was 19. She was the best thing that ever happened to me. We have four children and ten grandchildren and this year we celebrated our Golden Wedding surrounded by many family and friends. I am a lucky man.

BRIAN BALL

❝ I was 13 when I went into Barnardo's. My life hadn't been very pleasant up until then. But it wasn't until much later, when I went to collect my records, that I realised just how much Barnardo's had done for me.

REALISED

SKILLED

" My mother lost two husbands in the First World War and my sister and I were deserted. I spent my childhood in and out of orphanages.

At 14, I was sent to Goldings, a Barnardo's training school to learn a trade. Boys were given a choice and I learned sheet metal work. At the start of the Second World War, a team from De Havilland, a company making war aircraft, visited Goldings and selected four of the most skilled boys to join their workforce. I was one of them.

I worked there for a year. Barnardo's continued to support me financially. Then the factory was hit by four bombs from a German bomber killing 21 workers and injuring 70 people.

Fortunately, I escaped uninjured.

I was then ordered to work at the British Tabulating Company on one of the most important endeavours in defeating Nazi Germany — breaking *the Enigma code*. I was tasked with handcrafting and fitting all the metal components of dozens of 'Bombe' Enigma code machines. They successfully broke the code and ultimately turned the tide of the war.

I'm not an emotional bloke, but it's good to recognise what Barnardo's did.

ARTHUR DEAMER

REASSURING

"Mya was turning two when we started going to PIP (Barnardo's Parent and Infant Project). I have ongoing medical issues and was medically retired before Mya was born. After her birth, I started to lose confidence and was afraid to go out. I worried that I wouldn't be able to cope with the baby, as well as my condition, and we became housebound.

The first time walking into PIP was petrifying. We hadn't been out and Mya's pram was basically still brand new. The staff were very reassuring and there was no pressure. You could ask them anything and the support didn't stop when the session was over. They were always at the end of the

phone and they really went beyond the call of duty.

When Mya left to move on to nursery, I was asked if I would like to volunteer with the group and I jumped at it. It keeps me going out and I love working with the kids. I've been doing it for two years now. It also helps the other parents because I have their perspective.

PIP is so much more than just a playgroup. I couldn't speak highly enough about it. You come to them with no confidence, empty handed and asking for mercy – and they do anything they can to help.

ALISHA AND MYA BRIGGS, AGED 6

"After being in care and a period of being boarded out, I was transferred to Barnardo's training school, Goldings in Hertford. I found the regime strict but fair.

The confidence I gained there nutured me into my late teens. Whilst I did not know it at the time, Barnardo's provided me with the right 'keys to the door' enabling me to unlock life's challenges.

I left Barnardo's in 1961 and completed my full apprenticeship. I then had a number of other management roles until I joined the Crown Agents for Overseas Governments in the South Pacific. My life of travel had begun. Projects included: working

on a communications project in Iran; building major road bridges on St Vincent in the West Indies; developing new roads in Belize; and a major water project in Nigeria. I then returned to the UK and

studied at night school for a degree in Business Studies from my local polytechnic in Preston. During the day I was a senior building manager at my local hospital in Blackburn.

In 1993, I was appointed Chief Logistics Officer to the UN in the former Yugoslavia during the major conflict there. This was my biggest challenge to date. I was thankful for my upbringing in Barnardo's, which always emphasised that you should listen, understand and learn – and then get people to act in a positive manner. All of this helped me to make a success of my role over nearly four years.

My team of multi-nationals was responsible for delivering logistical support for some 28,000

KEYS TO THE DOOR

troops, ensuring that they received fuel, food and supplies to undertake their peacekeeping role. The budget was approximately $3 million a week. It was a huge undertaking, a difficult but a wonderful experience, despite all the hardships and horrors seen.

After retiring from the UN, I joined BAE Systems as a managing consultant working on infrastructure projects in Samoa, Poland, Czech Republic, Mexico, Saudi Arabia and Australia.

The biggest decision I made on retiring was to reconsider my feelings from my years in care. These deliberations led me to contact Barnardo's again after 50 years. I am eternally grateful that

I did. I left care without any academic qualifications and Barnardo's provided me with the right discipline, understanding of others, self-reliance and to be honest with yourself and others.

I have travelled widely, gained a greater understanding of other cultures and hopefully become a better man because of these experiences.

I deem myself lucky to have had an amazing life made all the richer by having a wonderful wife and family – they have made my life's journey, to date, complete.

TERRY WHITEHEAD

RELIEVED

66 When I was nine, mum was diagnosed with fibromyalgia, which causes severe pain and stiffness in her muscles and joints.

Every morning I'd have to help mum get dressed, brush her hair and have a shower and take her downstairs. I'd make her tea and toast and a sandwich for later. At school I'd be tired and worried, thinking that if mum tried to get up and fell over, there would be no one there to help and she would lie there in pain until I got home.

Eventually she told a doctor about our situation. When I met other young carers through Barnardo's, it made me feel relieved. It didn't make me feel embarrassed to tell other people that I look after my mum, it just made me feel a lot better about myself.

MALIK, AGED 17

66 I grew up in The Village, Barkingside with 65 cottages filled with children. In 1958, the first married couple arrived at our cottage. I believe it was a trial. They treated the cottage home as their own: decorating it with pretty wallpaper to replace the brown painted walls and inviting us to call them mum and dad. It was amazing and a success and more married couples followed.

I became a society florist apprentice in 1964. I helped do the arrangements for debutantes' coming out parties; royal events; and society functions. I went on to set up my own floristry business, which I ran with my husband for 23 years. It was a national enterprise and our clients included P&O Cruise Ships, Mecca Leisure and Butlins.

I retired early in 2007, and since then I've had a second career doing charity work, which I love. I have run a Brownies' Group, I'm a Women's Institute speaker, I represent Barnardo's Old Boys and Girls and I help at a local hospice with all aspects of care. And just for fun, I am a British Red Hatter!

Barnardo's provided me with a solid foundation and gave me the confidence and strength to do what I have wanted to do with my life.

MARY GODFREY

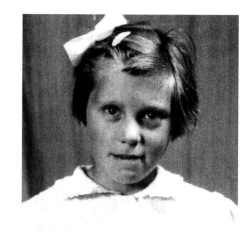

FOUNDATION

“Sometimes it's better going missing from home than being at home. I can't really think how many times I've been missing. The first time I disappeared from home I was 11. The longest period I have been gone is for two months. It was really difficult for me, I was really stressed, and I was scared. I had places to go, but I didn't trust the people.

BECKY (NAME CHANGED)

Barnardo's projects support and advise young people who are homeless and at risk of homelessness. It is estimated that around 83,000 homeless young people had to rely on councils and charities for a roof over their heads in 2014 (more than three times the official statistics) – according to Cambridge University's Centre for Housing and Planning Research.

Image posed by model

MISSING

INSTILLED

66 I think I've always had a real confidence and faith in myself, which was undoubtedly instilled in me by my foster mum Violet. She had to struggle to make the most of the straitened circumstances she found herself in during the post-war period in the North East.

As a young man, being ambitious was often considered to be 'bad form'. Yet when the people making key decisions about your future have very low expectations of you, it is crucial that you stand your ground and proclaim your worth.

I continue to work hard. I'm self-reliant and happy. I promote Barnardo's today because I can and there are so many other children and young people out there today desperately in need of support.

BRUCE OLDFIELD OBE, BARNARDO'S HONORARY VICE-PRESIDENT
Bruce was fostered with Violet Masters, a dressmaker from the age of 2 to 13 years. In 1971, the charity helped fund Bruce to attend a fashion and textiles degree course and in 1975 provided a £500 loan to help him set up his own company.

One of Britain's most successful fashion designers, Bruce is best known for his couture occasion wear and his clients have included: Barbra Streisand, Rihanna, Helen Mirren and Diana, Princess of Wales. He raises thousands of pounds each year in support of Barnardo's.

66 I have autism and have been coming to Dr B's Kitchen for two years. They have done brilliantly for me. I'm mostly a kitchen porter but they got me work experience at a restaurant – that was amazing. I'm starting work full time soon. Before Dr B's I wouldn't have talked to anyone, I would've been very shy. I had no confidence. I was bullied a bit at school. But now I'm really chatty. I'd like to keep working in restaurants and work my way up in the industry – I want to be a chef.

82

HARRY, AGED 19

Dr B's Kitchen is a café where young people with learning difficulties are supported and trained to develop the skills and professional qualifications they need to work in the catering industry.

BRILLIANTLY

SECURE

" Barnardo's taught me everything about life. To me it meant a regular meal. I saw the seaside for the first time because of them. I know how to use a knife and fork because they taught me. I felt secure because of them. They really mean so much to me.

When I was around six, I came into permanent care with Barnardo's. It felt like a proper home.

I was in lots of children's homes before Barnardo's. Mum had schizophrenia and couldn't look after me, so my most vivid memory as a child is of being hungry. My dad wasn't around, so I was left to look after myself.

I was good at football and used to play for a team run by the caretaker at Barnardo's. I got spotted by Fulham and taken on by them. The club also taught us another trade, as 90 per cent of professional footballers don't make it. Mine was hairdressing. Unfortunately, I got injured so became a hairdresser instead. I came third in the British Hairdressing Championships just after I'd trained and have gone on to own and run my own shop.

When I had my own children it brought up a lot of issues from my childhood and Barnardo's helped me with that. I've got a daughter and stepson and we're also raising a friend's child – her mum died and we'd promised that we'd always look after her – so we've got three children. Barnardo's has always been there for me.

JOHN SHEPPARD

> **"** I really like making the soup and I'm teaching other people how to do it now.

OWEN, AGED 19
Owen has learning difficulties.
He is diagnosed with global developmental delay.

1866

Thomas Barnardo arrives in London from Ireland.

1886

Disabled children trained in skilled work, such as boot making.

1871

Thomas Barnardo declares that no child is ever refused admission.

1900

Barnardo's is a national charity with 'ever open doors' nationwide.

The first 'Ragged School' for homeless children opens.

1867

1888

Barnardo's opens a lodging house for the children of prostitutes as protection from Jack the Ripper.

1885

Scarlet fever epidemic, but not one Barnardo's child dies.

The Children's Act
is passed.

1908

Barnardo's supports
Titanic orphans.

1912

Barnardo dies.
His state funeral is
attended by thousands.

1905

1920

Barnardo's reach
means the charity
is a household name.

World War One means
fewer funds and more
children in need of care.

1914

RESPITE

> 66 The family's involvement with Barnardo's started when Owen would spend a night or two away with another family. It helped Owen learn how to be away from me and gave me a respite break. I am responsible for all Owen's care needs on a day-to-day basis.
>
> At the project, Owen became one of the Three Chefeteers: learning how to make bread and soup through the service. This is something he really enjoys and he's teaching other students how to do it. He now has a placement in Tesco and is starting college in September.

MONICA, MUM

///// Timeline //////////////////////////////

1984

HRH Princess Diana becomes our President.

2013

Young carers and CSE work continues to expand.

2008

Barnardo's supports the campaign to end child poverty.

100,000 children helped every year.

2010

New work with the children of prisoners.

Barnardo's opens the UK's first female genital mutilation (FGM) prevention service.

2016

1995

Barnardo's pioneers child sexual exploitation (CSE) prevention.

World War Two. Social disruption
leads to a huge increase of children
in Barnardo's care. Evacuees and
Barnardo's children are given gas
masks and trained to take shelter.

1939

Barnardo's focus changes
towards supporting
whole families to stay
together.

1950

The state officially
takes responsibility
for children and the
NHS is established.

1948

1970

Barnardo's phases out
children's homes in favour
of fostering and adoption.

Voices of

RESILIENCE

FUTURE

66 When I was 12 or 13 years old I went down a bad path, I made a lot of wrong choices, taking drugs. I just got to a very low point. I didn't know what to do anymore and I wanted to take my own life. My past is very dark so it's very important to me that my future is very bright. I'll always remember my Barnardo's support worker, even if she has to leave my life. All I can see is the beauty in the world now, whereas before I had my child I could only see the bad.

JO

" After Krystallnacht* when I was 12 years old, my parents organised for my safe passage out of Germany. It was evidently pre-arranged that I would go to Barnardo's, but I have no idea by whom or when. I remember arriving at Liverpool Street station with hundreds of other Kindertransport children and my name being called out by Barnardo's. I was one of six girls taken to live in The Village, Barkingside.

I wrote letters to my parents. My mother was very out-going and I was very close to her. I still have the letters she wrote to me today. Once war broke out, the letters stopped.

I was very fortunate to have a very kind head teacher. We led a sheltered life at Barnardo's and I had no idea of the terrible things that were going on.

I am very grateful for the education I received through Barnardo's. In those days, you had to pay to stay on at school after 14 years and they knew I wanted to be a nurse.

My father survived and came to Britain after the war to see me. I discovered that my mother and all her family had been murdered in Auschwitz. I know he wanted me to return to Germany, but by now I was training as a nurse. I was very lonely, but had no intention of returning to Germany. Britain was my home and I became a British citizen as soon as I was old enough.

I am still very grateful to Barnardo's for all they did for me.

INGE BALL

Around 10,000 unaccompanied Jewish children were allowed out of Nazi Europe between 1938 and 1939. Inge Ball (formerly Fuss) was one of the Kindertransport children to be taken in by Barnardo's. She is pictured (centre) with her family.

*Krystallnact translates as 'night of broken glass' because of all the shattered glass that scattered after thousands of Jewish homes, businesses and synagogues were destroyed in organised Nazi pogroms across Europe on November 8 and 9 1938.

> Barnardo's has helped us a lot. Since we arrived in Northern Ireland, Marianne, our support worker, has taken care of everything. For the first three months she'd come to us every day and helped us register the children into a crèche, she arranged a bank account and cards, took us shopping. She comes and reads letters for us as well. Even now she'll come to help us, even if she has something important to do. I thank her – and Barnardo's – for what they have done.

In Syria we were right in the middle of the trouble. We could see the aeroplanes and hear the noise from the bombs. Now it's like we have been born again and we are getting into a new life step by step.

BASSEM, AGED 33

Bassem, his wife Rola and their children Maleik, Mousa and Mohammed fled their home in Syria after Bassem was kidnapped and tortured. The family were among the first group of refugees to arrive in Northern Ireland in December 2015 through the UK government's Vulnerable Person Relocation Scheme.

96

66 Hannah meant some day to drown herself. Blows, brutal kicks from heavy boots, semi-starvation: all these were hers. She knew what it was to be turned out of the squalid home at night with only one thin garment on to pass the hours 'til day as best she could, amid wet and cold.

The motherless Hannah had a father and brother, both brutal drunkards of the violent order. And viler conduct still, that may not be even named on these pages, fell to poor Hannah's lot.

So in April 1890, I came on the scene and it is now nearly 12 years ago since a new life, never before considered even possible to her, began for Hannah.

Home, sweet surroundings, good food and enough of it, warm clothing – in exchange for all that loathsome past. Imagine too, the wounds and bruises alike of body and mind that had to be healed.

One fine summer day she found herself with 86 other little damsels, her companions, on board the good ship bound for Canada.

Shortly after her arrival, Hannah was placed in a charming Christian home in the service of a medical man and his wife. Here our ladies who have the care and oversight of our girls in Canada regularly visited her.

No one would have recognised her as she attained her 19th year. Having received such constant professional care and such assiduous attention from her employers that she outgrew her delicacy and blossomed forth into vigorous health and beautiful womanhood.

HANNAH GLOVER

Quote by Thomas Barnardo from Barnardo's *National Waifs* magazine, 1902.

By the time Thomas Barnardo died in 1905, the charity he founded had opened 96 homes caring for more than 8,500 children.

During the 19th and 20th centuries, Barnardo's – along with many other childcare agencies – supported Government-backed schemes to send children to Canada and Australia to escape poverty and benefit from work opportunities in the British colonies. While Barnardo's did its best to support children in remote locations, it is now recognised that many children did not fare well as child migrants and these policies of the past have been discredited.

66 Nowadays it has become quite acceptable to wear one's Barnardo's past as a badge of honour. However my overriding emotion back then was not pride, but shame: shame that I did not know who my father was; shame in the manner my mother was living in; shame that as a Barnardo's boy, I was somehow different from my contemporaries.

I was a wartime baby and what little money there was, my mother spent on drink.

The next thing I knew, I was in Dr Barnardo's. There was no crying myself to sleep or anything like that. I suppose at such a young age, there was just too much for me to take in.

What I do remember was wanting to be treated just like any other child, rather than being stigmatised as a 'banana' (Barnardo's) boy.

In my case, I coped by reinventing myself, as I was always on the move. Each time I was presented with a new set of circumstances, I would adapt myself. My innermost thoughts and emotions were kept firmly tucked away.

To explain my situation was painful. And so I pursued my life, travelling the world and building up my exclusive travel company Jules Verne Voyages.

In 2012, one of my barges, the *Spirit of Chartwell* was chosen to carry the Queen and the royal family along the Thames at the Diamond Jubilee pageant. It felt that day like I'd been on a circular journey in life – a journey that began and has ended on the Thames.

PHILLIP MORRELL

101

“ I was desperate to leave school at 16, but when I did, I felt left behind by my friends.

I struggle with new people and can get very anxious and upset. It was very hard for me. Through Barnardo's Works, I got a work experience placement with Deeside Timberframe in Stonehaven. Barnardo's helped with my induction, helped with a mentor and much, much more. I started working two days a week and gradually built up to three.

In 2015, I was encouraged to apply to become a trainee design technician with the company – and was successful. I couldn't have done it without Barnardo's. They've been amazing.

CAMERON, AGED 19

AMAZING

STABLE

66 I came into Barnardo's care in 1954 when I was just four weeks old. My childhood was spent in a cottage at The Village, Barkingside with seven other children. I was brought up in a very loving and stable environment with two lovely housemothers known as Auntie Ann and Auntie Pearl. They gave me the confidence to live life as any other child despite only being 3' 8" tall.

Barnardo's supported me to do a college diploma in Office Routine. I was very fortunate to have work for 32 years and was able to buy my own flat.

I have many friends and have been lucky enough to have had many opportunities in life. I was even in *The Return of the Jedi*, one of the Star Wars films.

My aunties said that you only get out of life what you put in – and that is true. I have been very fortunate and have had, so far, a lovely life.

I am now retired and live in one of the Barnardo's cottages which has been developed into a retirement complex. I think I have come full circle!

LINDA BOWLEY

"I entered Barnardo's in July 1939 with my brother John and I was in various homes until I left school in December 1952. I was the youngest of six siblings in Barnardo's and we were all helped in different ways – teaching us trades, educating us, and preparing us for the world outside. They were our family in our time of need.

I was interested in electrical engineering and did an apprenticeship when I left Barnardo's but had to give it up after two years as I couldn't afford to live. I got paid £2 and 10 shillings a week and my board and lodgings was £2 and 5 shillings. During my National Service, I was in the army for three years in Germany and Libya.

I've had a very interesting life. I ended up working as a telephone engineer for the Post Office for 30 years – a job I loved. I've also been married for 53 years to a wonderful lady and her family are my family. I also have two sons and four grandchildren.

I think being a Barnardo's boy taught me to be resourceful. It taught me to work hard for a living. It makes you self-reliant.

DAVID GOODGER

LOOKED AFTER

"The NSPCC took us away when I was about seven. There were five of us and I only weighed 32lbs. I just remember someone coming in a big black car. Mother had gone out and left us, and they asked if we'd like to go for a drive. Of course, we said yes and they took us away. They looked after us in a holding place while they found mother.

Mother was sent to prison for neglect. I went to several Barnardo's homes before coming to The Village at Barkingside just after the war. When I left, I worked in a shop, then joined the NAAFI as a cook. I got married in 1955. I worked in a local factory and stayed for 18 years. I can't read that well and sometimes make mistakes when I write, but I went on to become shop steward, and then a convenor negotiating wages, so I did all right in life. I still live in Barkingside in sheltered housing and can see where I was brought up as a child.

DOROTHY THEOBALD

 When she was 18, my mother was thrown out of the house by her father because she was pregnant. We moved around until she died of TB in 1948. I was found in the room with her dead body.

I was sent to Barnardo's at Stepney, examined by a doctor and given clothes to wear. I remember the first night as my most frightening ever. I cried myself to sleep.

I was sent to the Boys Village Home in Woodford Bridge, with its lovely wee cottages. We had food – my first taste of mince and potatoes – and had a glass of milk before sleeping in our own beds, four to a room. It felt as if the sun had come out. We were treated like children and to me, at the time, it was the best place on earth.

I spent time in several homes and finally went to Goldings – a training school for boys to learn a trade – where I did printing and took to it like a duck to water.

When people ask me about Barnardo's, I say, to put it bluntly: 'they put a stick up my backbone and made me stand up straight'. Without these homes, children like me would have been lost. The older I get the more I appreciate what they did for me.

DAVID SWINGER

BACKBONE

“ I met him online and we met up two weeks later. I wasn't that happy at home and when I told him about it he completely listened. He said he was 18. I was only 12 so I felt really grown up, drinking, taking drugs. Turned out he was 26. He introduced me to other men. He said if I had sex with them, he'd give me money. He sent me all over the country to meet them. Over a year or so it got worse, more violent. I ended up in a psychiatric hospital.

Image posed by model

GREG, AGED 16 (NAME CHANGED)

Barnardo's is the largest provider of child sexual exploitation (CSE) support in the UK. We have worked with sexually exploited children and young people for more than 20 years, and have specialist services in over 40 locations.

EXPLOITATION

" I live in a flat provided by Barnardo's Leaving Care and I've been training as a waitress at Dr B's Kitchen. I'm about to leave and start my first job, which they helped me find. When I first arrived, I got upset a lot and would lose my temper because I had so much going on in my head. What I've learnt is that you just have to keep positive.

Without Barnardo's, life would be a whole load different. I've learnt so much and I enjoy every minute. Everyone is really supportive. All you have to do is ask. I would tell anyone to take the help and look on the bright side.

CHELSEA, AGED 19

William Mason was admitted to Barnardo's on 13th November 1889 and soon after joined the Royal Navy.

In June 1912, he wrote to Barnardo's from the *HMS Collingwood*, a dreadnought battleship built for the Royal Navy and launched in 1908.

His letter was published in *Jack Tar*, a Barnardo's magazine for all the boys who attended Watts Naval Training School in Elmham, Norfolk.

"I am glad to tell you we had the King down here a few days ago and we had a splendid time going to and fro out of Weymouth. I hope to see about the world by the time I have served 21 years and by that time I can just about call myself a sailor. I shall see the old school once again at Christmas, which I shall never forget all the time I am in the navy. That was the place where I learnt everything and which is helping me very much in this line of life."

WILLIAM MASON

Watts was a naval school in rural Norfolk, where boys aged 10 and upwards were sent to learn naval skills. The school, complete with its own land-locked ship and rigging, was open from 1903 to 1953.

113

HELPING

FAVOURITE

"I started living with my dad who had COPD* when I was 13 after my brother and sister had gone into care. I was his sole carer, doing the shopping, cleaning, helping him to hospital appointments...everything.

I was always the first to sign up for Barnardo's trips because I wanted to get away. At Indigo, David was by far my favourite worker.

He took me to West Ham matches. It was a big step for me because I hadn't seen them play since I was seven or eight. Both me and my dad had always loved them, but I couldn't go on my own. David always used to listen. He was one of the only people I could talk to about it. He was usually the driver when we went on trips and I would always sit at the front so I could speak to him."

115

KAI, AGED 19

David is one of Barnardo's longest serving volunteers at Indigo – a project which supports and empowers young carers.

*chronic obstructive pulmonary disease (COPD) – a family of lung diseases including emphysema and chronic bronchitis. Kai's dad passed away in 2015.

" We are identical twins and came into Barnardo's care when we were six months old. Our first home was Baby Castle in Scotland where we were looked after by Miss Bourne – she's in her nineties now and we still visit her.

We were taken to Barkingside to have an operation as we were both born with six fingers and six toes. We moved to another home in Bedford and then lived at Southborough Meadows. We had to leave Barnardo's when we were 16. Unfortunately we were badly treated in our first lodgings and Barnardo's came to our aid and arranged for us to stay with Mrs Knight. She couldn't cope with both of us, because we squabbled, so I left and Ian stayed with her – a great blessing for him as he stayed with Mrs Knight for 30 years.

Miss Bourne – another house mother – and Mrs Knight have been the backbone of our lives and I thank God that we were brought up in Dr Barnardo's Homes. Without Barnardo's, Ian and I would not have been able to live independent lives.

DAVID COCHRANE (QUOTED)
AND HIS BROTHER IAN

BLESSING

MEMORIES

My mum could turn her hand to anything – I've even got photos of her doing woodwork – and she learnt that in Barnardo's. She was taught silver service waiting as well. Mum had happy memories of her time in Barnardo's care. She got married in 1940 and had two children, but even when we were small, mum worked. In the early 1960s she passed her driving test and worked as a delivery driver. She loved driving around London. She was still working as a school dinner lady when she was in her 60s.

Mum didn't know much about her early life, just that she was 'illegitimate' and born in a slum area of Birmingham. She always kept in touch with her friends from Barnardo's.

She outlived all of them and was 98 when she died. Her determination, strength of character and love of life has been an inspiration to all our family. One of her granddaughters is now working in a Barnardo's shop!

RITA POOLE

Talking about her mother Ivy Earp who died in 2014 aged 98 years. Ivy is pictured in the above image on the far left.

66 After I left college, I was jobless for a long time. It was hard. When you have a job, you can find other jobs everywhere, but when you don't, no one will give you work. I didn't want my family to see that I'd sunk right to the bottom.

I saw a Barnardo's outreach worker in the street and she told me about their Talent Match programme. She was really supportive and helped me with my CV, looking for jobs, applications and a bit of financial support.

I began doing voluntary work one day a week, and I was encouraged to take a teaching qualification. I'm now working as a construction assistant at The Hub. I teach young people carpentry.

In 2015, I was highly commended in the *Young Builder of the Year* awards. Just to be there for the awards in the Houses of Parliament was one of the best experiences that I've had. With the right kind of support, anything is possible.

KHALED, AGED 23

The Hub is a Barnardo's project that provides training and apprenticeship opportunities in the construction and building industries.

COMMENDED

Voices of

LOYALTY

BRILLIANT

66 I enjoy helping my mum, but I go to my group every other week. We do lots of adventure things like climbing and canoeing. The school doesn't understand my situation – it's terrible – but Barnardo's is brilliant.

ABIGAIL, AGED 9

Abigail has attended Leicester CareFree young carers' service since she was six. Her mum Anna has MS (multiple sclerosis). Abigail is her main carer and gets up at 7am every day to help her mum and goes to bed at 9pm once her mum is settled. Last year, Abigail called an ambulance after her mother started choking. The paramedics said that Abigail's actions saved her mother's life.

There are at least 195,000 young carers in the UK.

66 I had one set of foster carers for the whole of my childhood in Barnardo's. They have always treated me as part of their family and that's what we do now.

Fostering means everything to me. I was lucky, so for me it's wonderful to give something back. Getting an MBE for fostering with my wife Mandy was completely unexpected to us. Going to Buckingham Palace to receive it was the proudest moment of my life.

124 We'd like to thank our own sons Dean and Glen, my Barnardo's foster parents Ada and Fred Goddard and all the foster children we've looked after over the years.

ROBERT GODDARD
Robert and his wife Mandy have fostered children for the last 23 years. During this time, they have cared for more than 65 children.

PROUDEST

REWARDING

66 Barnardo's recruited me as an appeals officer in 1961. I quickly found a home there and my grounding as a salesman helped me raise thousands of pounds for the charity, before I was promoted to appeals secretary.

The job was rewarding. It felt like we really achieved something for the children we supported. Barnardo's was a very good cause and I was proud to recommend them as an employer to the people I recruited.

Whilst often demanding, the work did have its perks. I twice met Barnardo's President of the time, Princess Margaret. On one of those occasions, I also had a brush with future rock royalty.

When I was in London to meet Princess Margaret, I stayed with Mr Jones, who was the public relations officer for Barnardo's children's homes in Stepney Causeway. I stayed in his son David's room for a week while he was away.

It only turned out that he would grow up and become known to millions of fans as David Bowie!

I loved every minute of my job and didn't want to retire and leave. I have many happy memories of my Barnardo's time.

FRED ASHTON
Fred died earlier this year aged 102.

WANT

66 When Riley was born, social services put a tag round him. I was really angry. They thought I was going to give my son a rubbish upbringing because my mum did, but you can't judge me for what my mum did. I want Riley to be respectful. I don't want him to go down the path I did, the way I behaved in my past or the way I've been brought up by my own mum. I want him to be independent and have a good life. I want him to do well at school and at college.

127

BECKY AND RILEY

Barnardo's runs a network of family centres with community-based parenting programmes across the UK to support parents with young children. Support includes: parenting groups, as well as one-to-one specialised work with parents who have particular needs.

34520
FRED HUMBY

LOSS

Fred Humby was 17 when he got a job as a pantryman on the Titanic – the largest liner in the world. Within three days of sailing, the liner sunk with the loss of more than 1,600 lives, including Fred's. Today it remains one of the most notorious and memorable naval tragedies of all time.

Fred grew up in Barnardo's care from the age of nine spending time at Watts Naval Training School in Norfolk.

"Frederick was not quite up to the physical standards required for the Royal Navy", said Barnardo's annual report in 1912, so instead he became a merchant seaman.

After Fred's death, Watts launched a memorial fund to raise money for a stained glass window to be erected in the young seaman's memory. "This, our first loss at sea, stirred the school deeply," said the school's newsletter. Sufficient money was raised and the window was duly created and erected, only to disappear after the naval school finally closed down in 1953. For years, the window's whereabouts was unknown, until it was rediscovered at a home in Texas in the 1980s.

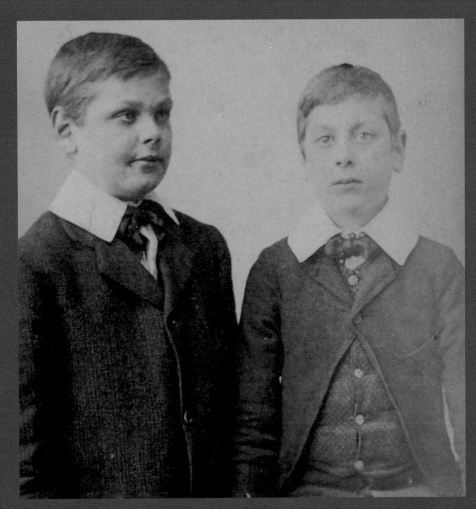

FRED HUMBY, 1885-1912

Sadly, the Titanic was linked with
Barnardo's in another way – many
children were left orphaned. Two boys
are known to have been admitted to
Barnardo's at Southampton in 1912 as
a direct result of the disaster: Harry
(9) and James Lang (5). The boys'
father, a 30-year-old coal trimmer,
went down on the Titanic and their
mother, who was paralysed from two
strokes was unable to care for them.

“ I was adopted through Barnardo's in 1957 to a loving family when I was six months old. I felt 100 per cent special. I am now head of a family law department and I represent children going through very difficult times. It might be adoption, care proceedings or arranging contact time between parents. There are so many very stressed and distressed children out there through no fault of their own. I was one of the lucky ones and children need a voice.

VAL COX

REPRESENT

GIVE BACK

66 From the time of my mother's death, shortly after my birth, I was unloved and unwanted. In 1950, I was taken into Barnardo's, having been locked in a bedroom on a very cold day for several hours with no food, water or heating.

At Barnardo's, where I stayed for the next nine years, I had a warm bed, I learnt a trade and gathered my best childhood memories.

As an adult, I've been married twice, have a lovely daughter and two grandchildren. I've always worked and have competed in disabled sport winning the British Polio Fellowship National Sportsman of the Year three times in the 1980s. I was also an active member of Gingerbread, the national association for one-parent families, and later became a member of their national executive.

I am also a member of the National Council for Old Boys and Girls at Barnardo's. It helps to give back a little of what I have been given – not just for my years in Barnardo's but for my achievements later in life. I know I am a better person for the experience.

ALAN DEARMAN
Alan died earlier this year.

PROUD

66 I tended to be a bit of a loner because of how things were with my family. The matron of my last home gave me the chickens to look after, because I loved animals. I used to cook the potato peelings overnight for the chickens in the Aga. The matron taught us all Scottish dancing and she taught me how to knit and I still make things today. I've knitted clothes for all my children and grandchildren.

I felt proud to be a Barnardo's girl because they always looked after you – without Barnardo's I didn't have a home at all and I was happy there.

DIANE MILLER

❝ I'd never been to Wimbledon, but loved watching it. It looks so big on the TV screen.

My favourite player is Serena Williams – her technique is amazing and she's really athletic. I remember being a little girl and screaming my head off when I watched her win in 2010. I imagined that I was there with thousands of people watching me and being really excited.

When I was asked to toss the coin at the Ladies' Final in 2016, I can't explain how happy I was. I was over the moon. Just to go to Wimbledon was amazing enough, but to be on Centre Court and get to flip the coin was just incredible.

I live with my mum and my aunt, who both have multiple sclerosis. My aunt is in a wheelchair and my mum is tired all the time, so she can't do much and we don't really go out. I have to help look after them both.

I was eight when I first started going to Barnardo's. We do all sorts of activities and go on day trips, and it's really fun, but Wimbledon is the best yet!

UMA, AGED 11

INCREDIBLE

66 I was in Barnardo's from ten months and stayed there all my childhood.

When I was growing up – everything was wonderful. I can't explain it. I loved the children's parties, the trips we went on – we were very well looked after.

I liked children and so when a job came up to work in the nurses' school, I leapt at the chance. I used to work with the pre-school children. I had to retire when I was 42 due to back problems, but I loved every minute of it.

Barnardo's has been a part of my life for all my life and I will always be part of the Barnardo's family.

DIANA REYNOLDS

PURPOSE

136

66 Foster care was one of
the most rewarding things
we ever did, and it gave us
a purpose to get up in the
morning. Support was always
available from Barnardo's if we
needed it and we were always
in close contact with other
carers. It's a fantastic service.

Life-long friendships are
established and we still
keep in touch with many of
the families long after their
children have grown up.

PAT COYNE

66 Our late son had cerebral palsy. Providing short breaks to other parents seemed a nice way for the two of us to work together in our own home. There was absolutely nothing like this kind of service when we were younger.

A short break gives parents some valuable time to care for their other children, who can sometimes be left out due to the demands of looking after a disabled sibling.

Our own children have benefitted as well. They've gained a greater understanding of what some other people have to go through. You definitely need a sense of humour, a lot of patience and a lot of love, but all of the children have a special place in our hearts.

PETER COYNE

Peter and Pat Coyne recently retired after providing short-breaks foster care to dozens of children and young people for almost 30 years. They are currently the longest-serving foster carers with Barnardo's Midlands Overnight Short Breaks.

66 I was admitted to Barnardo's when I was about three. It was me, my two older sisters and an older brother. My mother and father had a difficult marriage and split several times. Barnardo's tried to help them reconcile and they had my younger brother but it didn't work out. As far as I'm concerned, if I hadn't been in Barnardo's care I don't know where I would have ended up. I always thought that one day I would do something to pay them back for caring for me at such a vulnerable age. I fundraise, do talks and if someone in my area needs help, Barnardo's asks me to get in touch. I'm part of the National Council and if they ask me to do something to help, invariably I never refuse, because I was never refused as a child.

MO HARRIS

“ I was sent to Australia in 1950 when I was 13 years old. We had to be healthy and have a certain IQ to be accepted as child migrants. The boys were then sent to work on farms and the girls were domestic servants.

I've met these people and some of them are never going to get rid of their anger. For migrants with some other agencies, it was just so terrible. Thankfully a lot of the boys got off the farms and have done some really tremendous things.

I was a trustee at Barnardo's Australia for over eight years, a director for 12 years and I now joint edit the Old Boys and Girls magazine, organise reunions and generally keep in touch.

I don't feel that I've got to give the charity something back, I just like the people. I've been with them since 1941 and we all have this terrific rapport.

Marking Barnardo's 150th anniversary makes me think of all the wonderful dedicated people over the years who have looked after us and to whom it was not just a job, but a loving occupation.

Now we'd do anything to keep families together, but when I see some kids today, I don't think the homes were such a bad idea. At least you had somewhere to go at night and you had your friends. There was an invisible fence: you couldn't do this, that and the other.

SHIRLEY RONGE, CHILD MIGRANT
After Care worker for child migrants at Barnardo's Australia.

139

DEDICATED

66 I was entered into the Barnardo's system – together with my brother Arthur in 1940, and was very fortunate to spend many happy years at the lovely home at Ifield Hall from 1940 to 1954.

The home superintendent was strict but very fair. We had the luxury of games fields, a swimming pool and orchards. If, and when, we got into trouble we had to wash socks for a week – 150 pairs!

I can honestly say we had good treatment – food, heating and clothing – what more could you ask for during World War Two? I feel grateful thanks to a superb organisation.

JOHN WHELAN

FORTUNATE

66 My mother Lily was born in 1926 in Sutton-in-Ashfield. She was one of five children: three boys and two girls, and her father worked in the mines. He gambled and drank which left little money for food. The conditions were very bad and he was reported. Both girls were placed in Barnardo's, but I'm not sure what became of the boys. Mum's sister Winnie was placed with a loving family, but mum was fostered out and they didn't treat her very well. I think she ended up back at Barkingside.

When mum was older she found Winnie (pictured together top right) and they stayed in touch until mum passed away in 2000. Barnardo's saved my mum and I'm so grateful to them.

JUNE BOBY
June is pictured bottom right with her mum Lily Waspe

SAVED

ACTUALLY

" When my mum was pregnant with my little brother Ben, her pelvis dislodged and never repaired itself, so she had to go on crutches. She also has really bad arthritis. Because of the stress of not being able to look after her children, she's had lots of minor strokes, which has made her have memory loss. She struggles to get words out.

I first came to Barnardo's with my sister seven years ago. I've grown up with some of the people here. When I come these days, it's like being at a friend's house. It's nice to come somewhere where you can tell people things and they actually do understand.

LORETTA, AGED 14

Voices of

ADVENTURE

" I was 14 when I went into Barnardo's and although I was only in care for a couple of years, I always remember my time there.

On arrival, I was told that once you are a Barnardo's boy, you are always a Barnardo's boy, and that stayed with me. For someone like me, who had no family and no home, that was a major thing. It was my identity and still is.

Barnardo's was there for me. My welfare officer, Mr Andrews, was extremely kind and helped me for many years. I remember when I was about 25 and had nowhere to stay, he found me a bed back at the home until I got back on my feet again.

IDENTITY

KLAUS ARMSTRONG-BRAUN
Klaus was born in Germany in 1940
to a Polish mother and a German
father. Both his parents were killed
during the Second World War. Klaus
was taken to Ireland by the Red
Cross as a refugee when he was
four. Over the next ten years, he
lived with 13 different families often
facing extreme prejudice because
of his German heritage. In 1954, at
the age of 14, Klaus was moved to a
Barnardo's home in England. As an
adult, he settled in the same town as
his Barnardo's home and became a
county and town councilor. He is also
a keen local environmentalist and is
committed to protecting ecosystems
for future generations.

BREAK

" I started going to Barnardo's Saturday Club* when I was six, so I have been going for six years.

It's difficult for me to go to other after school clubs. I really look forward to going and it gives me two hours of freedom and a break from my parents!

I like it because they know me so well there and they know I don't like things like balloons, so they never have them.

There are lots of different people and things to do like clay, music, drums and a microphone. I play tennis with Big Andrew and I look forward to seeing him and we talk about rugby and motorbikes. We also go on outings to places like Ark Farm and Mosside Leisure Centre.

It's good there's a club like the Saturday Club, otherwise I would just stay at home and be bored. It's important to me and I will miss it when I don't go anymore.

TOBY, AGED 12
Toby, who is on the autistic spectrum, also has ADHD and complex learning difficulties.

*Play For All, Bangor Saturday Club, is for children with learning difficulties, medical conditions and sensory impairments.

He lived in the other half and it was where he kept racehorses, so we used to watch the horses galloping past.

I moved to Goldings training school when I was 14 and trained to be a lathe user. I also got to be a ball boy at Wimbledon. I was on Centre Court for the final, which was won by Yvon Petra, the Frenchman.

66 I went to Stepney (Barnardo's headquarters in East London) when I was 11. I had my hair combed for nits and then was moved to Essex to have my tonsils out.

It was 1941 and being wartime Lord Derby let Barnardo's use half his home – Stanley House.

Wimbledon was very different then to how it is now. Very austere. I guess it was just after the war. I did enjoy the strawberries and cream though. They were a real treat, especially as we had no bananas or oranges during the war.

PETER KNIGHT
For 20 years, from 1946 to 1966, Barnardo's provided ball boys for the Wimbledon championships at the All England Lawn Tennis Club.

TREAT

FAMILY

66 I was born during World War One on 8 March 1916. I was taken into Barnardo's and was boarded out with a family in Suffolk who had eight children and treated me as one of the family.

At 11, I was transferred to Barnardo's Russell Cotes Naval School, where boys were trained as merchant seamen. We were known by a number, rather than by name. I didn't grow tall enough though to make the grade, so was transferred to Goldings to learn a trade. I wanted to become an engineer, but as there were not enough places, I trained as a boot maker.

I was offered the chance to go to Canada but missed the boat owing to a spell in hospital. In World War Two, I was conscripted and was taken as a prisoner of war by the Japanese in Java for three and a half years.

I married and had a family and, after the war, spent many years working in Australia as a boot maker before returning to England in 1988 to be with my family, who had come back before me.

Growing up, I had no family, only to discover when I was nearly 80 that I had three half-siblings and four first cousins! I'm very happy to have been fortunate enough to have descendants.

At my 100th birthday party recently, there were nearly 80 guests. I had three children, four grandchildren and eleven great-grandchildren. I feel I have been very lucky.

FRED HODGE

CLOSE

" I don't remember not being in Barnardo's – I was there from the age of one until I was nine. I lived in a Barnardo's home known as The Village and enjoyed it there; we were like a family unit with days out and holidays. We had live-in carers and Marjorie looked after me the entire time I was there. She passed away in 2002. I went to her funeral and she left me memorabilia in her will, that's how close we were.

I didn't feel prepared to leave, the only family I'd known was Barnardo's. Even the primary school was in The Village.

Taken from care to live with my family, as a nine-year-old, was a bit of a nightmare. I hardly knew them. It's quite a disjointed family. For our early childhoods, most of my brothers and sisters weren't raised together.

In my early 20s, I developed an interest in music technology and drifted into various recording projects and musical theatre. I just immersed myself in it. People kept asking me to record stuff and, as so often happens in life, one project can get sidetracked, and blossom into something unexpected. Such circumstances led to me spending much of 1994 in the studio with Geordie duo Ant and Dec. I wrote *Let's Get Ready To Rhumble* while working with them on their first album.

There are no longer any children in care at The Village. There are shops and houses now where I used to run around and play. I have great memories of my time there.

MICHAEL OLTON MCCOLLIN

Tom Bishop was born in Edinburgh on 6 August 1885 and admitted to Barnardo's when he was ten years old. Later that year, he and his brother Robert were migrated to Canada.

Initially they were sent to live with a farming family in southern Ontario. As soon as they saved enough money to pay off their passage, they headed west to Alberta. In 1908, it was believed to be 'the land of golden opportunity'.

However, when they got there, the brothers found many settlers had gone broke and were looking to leave or sell up. Tom and Robert eventually sought to return 'home' too.

They undertook a long journey 'riding the rods' back to Canada – travelling in and under empty box cars. En route, Tom took a horse training course. He quickly gained a reputation for successfully mastering difficult horses.

Tom was a founding member of the Western Horse Association of Ontario, which promoted the western style of riding and the spirit of the west.

In 1914 Tom received an invitation to put on a "trained horse exhibition and wild west display" to raise money for the troops of the First World War.

OPPORTUNITY

grandfather's footsteps, and still produce wild west shows; are stunt riders in films and shows; and ride in rodeo shows (see Tom's family today pictured left).

In 1965, Tom's son and daughter came to England with their horses and were part of the Lancashire fairgrounds that summer – bringing a little of the wild west to northern England.

The Wild West Show is still in existence today. Having been running since 1914, it is the oldest Wild West show in Canada, and so one of the oldest in the world.

The show was a great success and many more followed, nearly all of them culminating with a performance of Tom's horse Saladin.

Tom later married Eva, his business secretary, and they had two children followed by three grandchildren. They have all followed in their

TOM BISHOP

INDEPENDENTLY

ISAAC, AGED 21

Isaac has severe physical
limitations. He uses a mobility chair
and operates his computers and
video games with his feet by lying
on the floor. He is pictured here
with his Olympic torch.

" Barnardo's should generate more attention around the work it does with disabled people. From the age of five, I had a sleepover at their Indigo project on the first Monday of the month for about eight years. It was great as we went and did different activities.

I finished sixth form three years ago and am now doing film and media independently. I was going to study film at college but didn't as I've already done a lot of what they were teaching in my A Levels. I completed an internship in film for a charity and helped Barnardo's make a video for their Corporate Audit and Inspection Unit (CAIU).

Last year I completed a 14,000ft sky dive. I found a company in Ohio that had the right harness for me, as I couldn't do it in the UK. It was my first time out of Europe so that was two major experiences in one.

I've got my own camera. I want to start filming where I go and how I do things to show people how hard or easy some day-to-day activities are and with this I want to inspire people.

I carried the Olympic Torch for London 2012 Olympics during its relay around the UK – I got to keep the torch too. It's now displayed in a trophy stand in my room.

Thank you Barnardo's for this journey. It has been very helpful and something I can take on into my future.

66 My childhood was over in 24 hours once I reached 16. I was in a children's unit, then homeless, then I was moved into a B&B, then into a flat – all in the space of seven days. It had a big impact on my mental health. I had no one to support me.

I was then referred to Barnardo's Scotland. They've taught me the life skills I need. I had no idea about living on my own and running a house.

I would like to help young people from all different backgrounds. I've been taking notes and I'm putting them in to a book about being in care; leaving care; moving on into adulthood and into a career. My plan is to write the book when I'm 21 to document the journey to help other young care leavers.

Barnardo's Scotland was only in my life for a short time – one year and three months – but I'll remember them for a very long time. They had a huge impact.

I'm now going to do some fundraising for the charity to try and return the favour. That's my goal for this year.

ANDREW, AGED 19

Andrew left school at 15 with no qualifications, and at the time was undiagnosed as being dyslexic.

Through Youth Housing Support, 16+ and Learning Hub, Andrew has secured six qualifications. He now chairs the local youth forum and represents North Lanarkshire covering Wishaw, Shotts and Motherwell. He is going to stand as a Member of the Scottish Youth Parliament.

LIFE-SKILLS

"I was the oldest of five children. We grew up in inner Belfast and my mother died when I was four years old. Our father looked after us for the next two years and then we were taken in by Barnardo's.

I remember that first night lying in bed with the moon shining in and not knowing what I was going to waken to, but we had been lifted out of Belfast to somewhere that felt like heaven. We felt cared for.

I will always be grateful to Barnardo's. The people who looked after me had a big influence on my life. Next year my wife Eileen and I will celebrate our 50th wedding anniversary. We had two boys and now we have seven grandchildren and every year we take them to Orlando

Disney World. I owe Barnardo's everything. If I hadn't gone into Barnardo's I don't know where my life would have gone, but it worked for me.

JIMMY KENNEDY

MARVELLOUS

 I went into care because my parents were miserably poor.

My first ten years in Barnardo's were nothing but sheer hell as my house parents were horrible to us. From 1944 though, everything was right. We had new house parents and they were absolutely marvellous.

I was encouraged to have aspirations and ambitions. I remember being taken to see Barnardo's Chief Executive and told to go back and finish my Chartered Secretary examinations. They agreed to pay for my digs and college costs for a year and a half.

I later became company secretary at several multi-national companies including the Middle East Economic Digest – the leading authority on politics in the Middle East.

I remained close to my two brothers throughout my life (pictured with John in Barnardo's) but had no relationship with my mother.

JOHN WEST

GLOW

" As a small child, I spent time in Barnardo's.

When I was four, I was adopted and there my happiness ended. When my adoptive father returned from war it was a terrible shock to me and I took an instant dislike to him. Rightly so, for he would beat me for the smallest thing with a lump of wood, metal or leather.

One of the things that affected me most was that I longed for a hug. No one cared for me.

When I was 18, I was called up for National Service. This was the beginning of a life without a father I was so afraid of, and of a stepmother (his second wife), whom I hated.

It was at this time that I thought about Barnardo's.

They were the happiest days of my childhood. I wanted to repay them in some way. Today I have raised in excess of £132,000 through talks, donations and fundraising.

Every time I hear the word Barnardo's I get a glow inside.

Barnardo's has helped so many young people, who otherwise would not have survived or had a chance. Barnardo's works tirelessly, quietly and with purpose.

KEITH WALLER

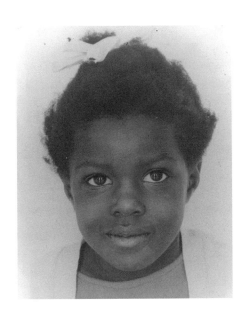

money so I could sit still, be cross-legged and quiet.

I laughed, and I realised that the gift Barnardo's gave me was faith. There were people who gave up their life to work for Jesus. I was touched by faith, when I was seven. I became friends with a little girl called Anne who was playing in the sandpit in between our cottages. She told me she was going to die because she had a hole in her heart. She often smiled saying: 'I'm moving to heaven and will live with the angels'. There was an unnerving calm, a radiance and beauty I could never forget. She could live and die because she had faith.

Barnardo's culture of faith saved my life. I found liberation from the labels 'Gruesome',

'Rubber Lips' and 'Blacky' that were foisted upon me during my childhood, by placing the Buddhist teachings at the centre of my life.

VALERIE MASON-JOHN

“ Twenty years ago I was standing in the sunshine outside a shrine room, where I had been meditating for the past hour. And these thoughts leapt across my mind: 'How did I end up here?' I hated sitting cross-legged as a child in assemblies at Mossford Village school. And now I was paying

FAITH

Afterword

66 We all seek inspiration and hope in life and *Barnardo's Voices* is full of such stories. We hope you have enjoyed them.

In my experience most people believe that every child has the potential to be wonderful and do wonderful things. Tragically, as the stories in this book show, some children are damaged or severely disadvantaged before they can even make a start in life. That's why Barnardo's is so important. We truly *Believe in Children* and the better futures they can all have with the right help.

During my time as a Barnardo's Trustee every child and Barnardo's worker I've met has strengthened my belief in how precious these children are and how we mustn't let them down. Whatever support we give, we want to be there for them as long as we are needed.

Since Barnardo's was founded in 1866 there has always been demand for our work and it continues to grow. We know there are thousands upon thousands of children today whose lives may be seriously damaged or whose opportunities will be undermined without the care and support they desperately need. How can we do more to help?

Over the next ten years we have ambitious plans to increase the number of children we work with and to provide support in more depth where it is needed. We rely heavily upon the money we receive from supporters to make this happen. Whether it is a one-off contribution, a monthly direct debit, a donation to one of our shops or leaving a gift in a Will – all of them mean we can target funds where they are needed most.

Donations enable us to identify and respond to really difficult issues before they are widely recognised, such as child sexual exploitation or the often ignored needs of the children of prisoners. They are vital for our ability to develop new projects with the potential to improve the lives of thousands of children.

165

The longer I have volunteered to work for Barnardo's the more I realise how our work today is consistent with the mission that inspired Thomas Barnardo 150 years ago. But it takes time and money to transform lives and you make that possible. Your gifts help us to help others.

Thank you for your generosity and for your belief in children. Thank you too for helping us mark our achievements on our 150th anniversary. We look forward to sharing the journey together to help all our children in the years ahead.

TONY COHEN, CHAIR OF TRUSTEES BARNARDO'S

Index

Thank you so much to everyone who has contributed to this book and helped to tell the story of the impact Barnardo's has had in transforming the lives of some of the UK's most vulnerable children and their families over the last 150 years.

We would like to thank all of the children and members of their families, as well as Barnardo's staff and volunteers, from both the past and the present, who have provided such powerful words, photographs and stories as a testament to the work of the charity.

In particular, we would like to acknowledge and thank Diane Church, Alison Blaxland, David O'Sullivan, Francesca Bray, Jonathan Jacques, Lisa Hasler, Paul Beard, Maureen Jeffers, Nina Clarke, Martine King, Zena Ambrose, Faith Orr, Ann Cattini, Lydia Rodrigues, Caroline Baker, A J Woods, Emma Marchant, Hayley Wellfair and the office of our patron Her Majesty The Queen for providing the Foreword.

Thanks to Cambridge Jones, *Homes & Property* magazine, our ambassador Baroness Floella Benjamin and the *Chester Chronicle* for the portrait photographs they provided of Bruce Oldfield OBE, Philip Morrell, John Sheppard and Klaus Amstrong-Braun respectively.

THANK YOU

Help give a vulnerable child someone to turn to. Leave a gift in your Will to Barnardo's.

www.barnardos.org.uk/giftsinwills
020 8498 7880